ABSOLUTE BEGIN

ALTO
Saxophone

WISE PUBLICATIONS
London/New York/Paris/Sydney/Copenhagen/Madrid

Exclusive Distributors:
Music Sales Limited
8/9 Frith Street,
London W1V 5TZ, England.

Music Sales Corporation
257 Park Avenue South
New York
NY10010, USA.

Music Sales Pty Limited
120 Rothschild Avenue,
Rosebery, NSW 2018,
Australia.

Order No. AM92620
ISBN 0-7119-7432-2
This book © Copyright 1999 by Wise Publications

Arranged by Steve Tayton
Cover and text photographs by George Taylor
Other photographs courtesy of LFI/Redferns
Book design by Chloë Alexander
Model: Gavin Stewart

Printed in the United Kingdom by Printwise (Haverhill) Limited,
Haverhill, Suffolk.

Your Guarantee of Quality:
As publishers, we strive to produce every book to the highest
commercial standards. This book has been carefully designed to
minimise awkward page turns and to make playing from it a real
pleasure. Particular care has been given to specifying acid-free,
neutral-sized paper made from pulps which have not been
elemental chlorine bleached. This pulp is from farmed sustainable
forests and was produced with special regard for the environment.
Throughout, the printing and binding have been planned to ensure
a sturdy, attractive publication which should give years of
enjoyment. If your copy fails to meet our high standards, please
inform us and we will gladly replace it.

Music Sales' complete catalogue describes thousands of titles
and is available in full colour sections by subject, direct from Music
Sales Limited. Please state your areas of interest and send
a cheque/postal order for £1.50 for postage to:
Music Sales Limited, Newmarket Road, Bury St. Edmunds,
Suffolk IP33 3YB.

Enhanced CD
The audio on the accompanying Enhanced CD can be played on
either your hi-fi or multimedia PC. If you are on the Internet and
want to browse the world's largest selection of sheet music, simply
place the CD in your CD-Rom drive and follow the on-screen
instructions.

Contents

Introduction

Welcome to Absolute Beginners for Alto Saxophone. The Alto Sax remains one of the world's most popular instruments – this book will guide you from the very first time you take your sax out of its case, right through to playing your first song.

Easy-to-follow instructions
will guide you through

• how to assemble and look after your sax
• finding your first notes
• reading basic notation
• playing your first sax pieces

Play along with the backing track as you learn – the specially recorded audio will let you hear how the music *should* sound – then try playing the part yourself.

Practise regularly and often. Twenty minutes every day is far better than two hours at the weekend with nothing in between. Not only are you training your brain to understand how to play the saxophone, you are also teaching your muscles to memorise certain repeated actions.

At the back of this book you'll find a section introducing some of the music available for saxophone. It will guide you to exactly the kind of music you want to play – whether it's a comprehensive tutorial series, rock, jazz or blues, easy-to-play tunes or "off the record" transcriptions, there's something there for all tastes.

Mouthpiece

Key Guide

Crook

Key Screw

Tension Screw

Octave Key

Thumb rest/support (back)

Strap ring (back)

Thumb hook (back)

Rollers

Key Guard

Ligature

Palm Keys

Key Pearls

Table Keys

Bell rim

Bell

Bell Brace

Key Guard

Bow

Bow Cap

What's in the case?

It's important to follow the assembling procedures carefully. Your case should contain the following:

1 A sling/neck strap, etc.

2 The main body of the saxophone.

3 The crook (with cork around one end).

4 A mouthpiece.

5 The ligature (which holds the reed onto the mouthpiece).

6 The mouthpiece cap.

7 An end stopper (known as a bung – not shown).

8 A box of reeds – medium soft, strength 2 (always have extra reeds on hand).

Cork grease and cleaning accessories should also be in the case. Before proceeding, familiarise yourself with the names of all the different parts.

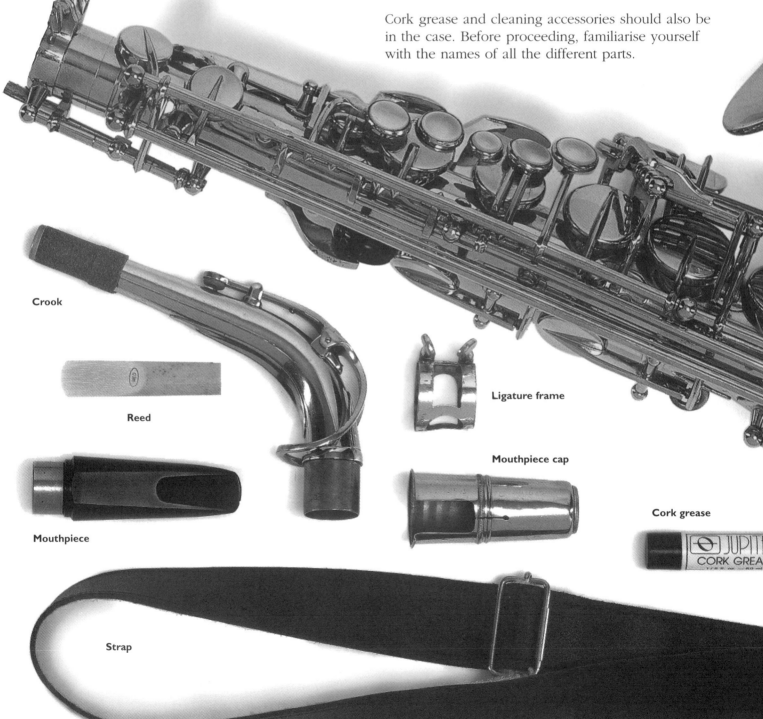

Crook

Reed

Mouthpiece

Ligature frame

Mouthpiece cap

Cork grease

JUPITER CORK GREASE

Strap

Metal mouthpiece cap   **Reed**   **Metal screws**   **Cork**

Here's how the mouthpiece, cap and crook fit together.

Now let's assemble your saxophone!

The reed and mouthpiece

1 Checking And Moistening The Reed

Take one medium soft reed (strength 2) from the box. Check it has no splits or chips (which usually occur at the tip). Place the thin half of the reed in your mouth and soak it with saliva. The tip of the reed must be moistened thoroughly before use.

Tip

Make sure you only handle the reed by the thick end, not the fragile thin end.

2 Preparing The Mouthpiece

With the reed still in your mouth, remove the mouthpiece cap from the mouthpiece and gently loosen the screw (or screws) that you will find on the side of the ligature. Remove the ligature from the mouthpiece by sliding it upwards.

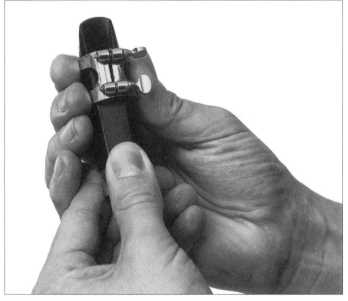

3 Placing The Reed

Gently place the moistened reed on the mouthpiece, flat surface downwards, with the thinnest part on the tip of the mouthpiece. Place it exactly in line with the top edge of the mouthpiece, as shown.

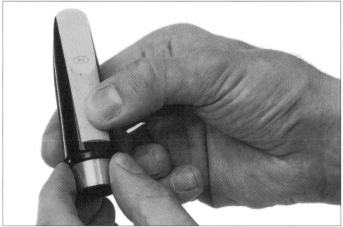

4 Securing The Reed

Pull the ligature back over the reed until all three components (ligature, reed and mouthpiece) are in position.

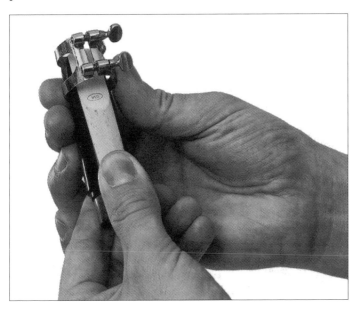

6 Connecting The Mouthpiece To The Crook

Take both the crook and the cork grease and coat the cork with lubricant.

Cork grease should be applied to the crook only when the mouthpiece will not slide easily on to it. (Once a week with regular playing).

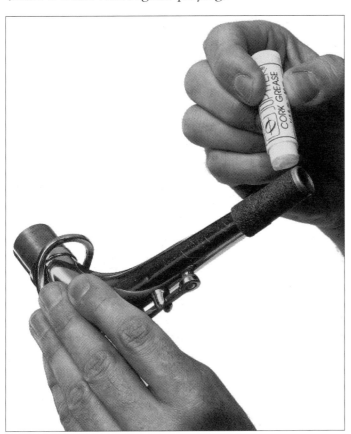

5 Tighten The Screw

Tighten the ligature screws until finger tight. The reed should be held firmly, but not too tightly, by the ligature. Finally, carefully replace the mouthpiece cover, minding the tip.

Take the completed mouthpiece unit and place it on the crook. Gently twist it from side to side until it covers roughly half the cork. Put your mouthpiece and crook back into your case.

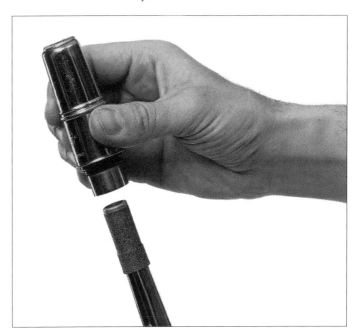

Tip

Always keep the mouthpiece cover in your pocket while playing and replace it as soon as you finish. Most reed accidents are caused by careless handling, either before or after playing.

Putting it all together

7 Connecting The Crook To The Main Body

Place the sling around your neck. Placing your right hand in the bell, pick up the main body of the instrument and support the saxophone in an upright position resting on the bottom of the case. Remove the bung and loosen the tension screw.

Bung ——

Now, taking the combined crook and mouthpiece unit, gently but firmly insert the open end of the crook into the top of the main instrument body. Listen for the soft click indicating that the crook is firmly connected.

Adjust the crook and tighten the tension screw until finger tight.

8 Connecting The Sling

Look at the back of the main body of the saxophone. About half way down you will find a small ring. Connect the sling hook to this ring.

Now lift the whole saxophone out of the case, step back and allow the sling to take the full weight of the instrument.

Important: Never pick up the saxophone by the crook.

9 Holding Your Saxophone

Just below the sling hook you will see a thumb support for your right hand thumb. Look above the sling hook and you will find a thumb rest button for your left hand thumb. (This left hand position will enable you to use the octave key when necessary.)

With your hands in these positions gently grasp the main body and bring your saxophone into the upright position. Your neck should take most of the weight, but you may need to push out a little with your arms.

10 Adjusting The Sling

Adjust the sling so that the mouthpiece is parallel to your mouth. Do not bend your head down. With your head up and shoulders relaxed let the saxophone come comfortably to you.

Thumb rest/support

If you find you are having to bend your head forward to the mouthpiece, try adjusting the sling upwards.

Conversely, if the mouthpiece is too high, adjust the sling downwards.

The left hand operates the upper keys, the right hand operates the lower keys.

So there you have it! Ten easy steps for assembling your saxophone. Follow this routine in reverse when dismantling.

Tip

Always try to stand (or sit) with your head up, and with your arms, hands and fingers relaxed and held in a natural position. The quality of your playing will be affected by any stiffness in your body.

Your first note

Now, for the impatient... instant gratification! If you just can't wait another minute before playing your new saxophone, it's certainly understandable. So if you want to try your first note before going through all the correct procedures, now is the time.

Make sure you have assembled and set up your sax properly, then follow the instructions below to produce your first note. Don't be too disappointed if the results are not what you expect – it's not quite as easy as it looks!

You don't need to worry about pressing down any keys to produce a note – just support the instrument as shown in the photograph.

Breathing Is The Key

As you know, without a good supply of air your brain won't function, your hands and fingers won't move, and most importantly, without air your saxophone won't work!

Correct breathing is vital in order to play the saxophone. Although you've been breathing all your life, as a saxophonist you must use a special breathing technique.

Using Your Diaphragm

Your diaphragm is the long flat muscle situated at the bottom of your lungs. The easiest way to make yourself conscious of it is to cough: you will feel a ripple of muscle across your stomach – that's your diaphragm.

You'll need to use this same technique, but instead of a momentary contraction of the diaphragm, you're aiming for a prolonged contraction – like a long cough! This will enable you to create a controlled flow of air passing from your lungs into the saxophone.

It sounds very complicated but using this technique you'll produce a wonderfully full tone.

Tip

Practising in a standing position will help you to breathe properly.

Tip

Don't bend your head forward. Keep your head up and bring the mouthpiece up to your mouth. Support the mouthpiece and reed with your lower lip muscles, not your teeth.

1 Draw your lower lip lightly inwards over your bottom teeth.

2 Place a quarter of the mouthpiece (reed downwards) on the lower lip.

3 Rest your upper front teeth firmly on top of the mouthpiece. Don't bite your lower lip and don't raise your head.

4 Place your tongue on the reed tip.

5 Keep your shoulders low and inhale deeply through the corners of your mouth.

6 Gently but firmly close your lips around the mouthpiece to prevent air escaping from your mouth.

7 Now inflate your lungs from your diaphragm (not with a huge gulp, just slightly more than usual). Place your tongue tip gently on the reed and push with your diaphragm.

As soon as your diaphragm begins to push and you feel gentle air pressure in your mouth, release your tongue with a "Tu" attack. This is called tonguing.

Now that you know the correct routine for starting a note, have a go! Continue playing for as long as your breath will allow without discomfort, keeping the sound steady.

Don't breathe in through the mouthpiece – you won't get enough air and it makes a shocking noise! It is best not to puff out your cheeks either, as this will cause discomfort leading to a poor sound with no control of tone or volume.

Listen to **Track 1**, and then play the saxophone as you did before. The sound you just made should match that on the CD. (If not, try again!)

Well done! You have produced your first note. Now unhook your sax from the sling and put it down somewhere safe.

Tip

For best results don't empty your lungs completely before you take another breath.

Try to take a fresh supply of air (either through your nostrils or the sides of your mouth) without disturbing the position of the mouthpiece in your mouth.

CHECKPOINT

WHAT YOU'VE ACHIEVED SO FAR...

You can now:
- Assemble your saxophone
- Place your left and right hands correctly
- Use the correct mouth position
- Use diaphragm breathing

Finger positions

Using the enclosed fingering chart, compare the photos with your sax and try to find all the numbered keys that are illustrated on the chart.

Each of your fingers is given a number – if you remember that both your forefingers are index number 1 (L1 and R1) you can't go wrong.

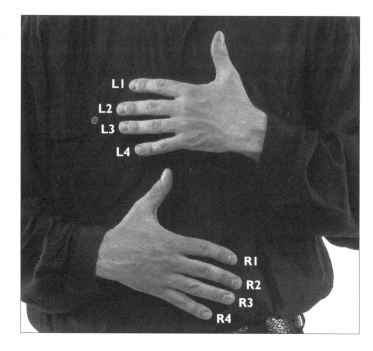

The Right Hand

Put your right hand thumb under the thumb hook and curl your hand around the instrument, placing R1, R2 and R3 just over the pearl finger cushions 1, 2, and 3 as shown in the photo below.

The Left Hand

Now curve your left hand around the sax with your thumb on the back thumb rest and place your fingers L1, L2 and L3 as shown in the photo below.

Your fingers L4 and R4 have a choice of keys – but more about this later. For now just hold the instrument and feel the balance – get comfortable and relax into it.

These are the main finger positions – soon you'll automatically rest your fingers above the correct keys without looking at them.

> ## Tip
>
> Starting with finger L1 press and hold down one key after another, going down the sax (L1, L2, L3 then R1, R2 and R3), then release them one by one in reverse order.

Music notation is a universal language written with symbols which indicate *pitch* (sound) and *rhythm* (pulse or beat).

The Stave (or Staff)
Notes are written on a series of five lines. This is called the *stave* (or staff).

The Clef
The first thing you will see on a stave is a *clef*. Different clefs are used for instruments that have different ranges – for example the piccolo and the trombone read music from staves with different clefs.

Both alto and tenor saxophones read music written in the *Treble Clef*.

Note Position On The Stave
So how can you tell which note is which?

Notes are named after the line or space on which they fall. The stave lines can be "extended" up or down using short lines called *leger lines*. Note heads can be written on these lines to write pitches.

At this stage there's no substitute for simply learning which note names correspond to which lines and spaces – however, you may find the following phrases/words help you to remember:

A Note On Transposition
Unlike pianos, violins and many other instruments, saxophones are transposing instruments, which means that music is written in a key or octave differing from their actual sound.

The E♭ alto saxophone actually sounds six notes lower (a major sixth interval) than the written pitch – so when you play C in the music, the note produced is actually E♭.

Likewise, the B♭ tenor saxophone transposes nine notes lower (a major ninth interval), so a written C would actually sound B♭.

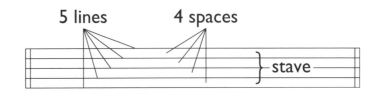

5 lines   4 spaces

} stave

Treble Clef

Jargon Buster

Pitch – how high or low a note is
Beat – the basic pulse of music
Clef – sign that appears at the start of the stave

These notes sound lower than these notes

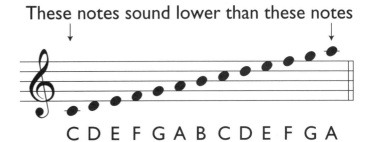

C D E F G A B C D E F G A

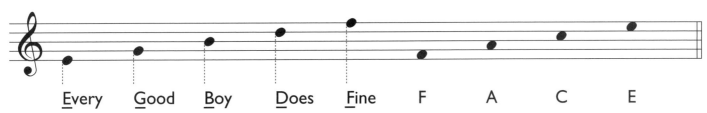

Every   Good   Boy   Does   Fine   F   A   C   E

Written:

Sounds:

Rhythm

Notes don't just tell you about pitch – they also give you information about *duration*. We can indicate different durations in different ways – by adding a *stem* or *tail* to a note, or by filling in the note head:

o   **Semibreve**
(Whole note)

♩   **Minim**
(Half note)

♩   **Crotchet**
(Quarter note)

♪   **Quaver**
(Eighth note)

♪   **Semiquaver**
(Sixteenth note)

You can think of rhythm as the sound of a melody played on a drum – without pitch. Rhythm gives the feeling of movement in music and its basic unit is called a beat (or pulse). Beats usually remain steady throughout a piece of music.

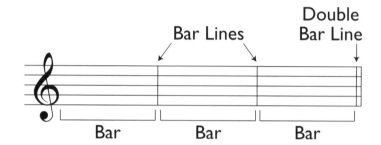

Bars and Bar Lines
To make music easier to read, the stave is divided into *bars* by vertical lines called *bar lines*.
At the end of a piece or a section of music you will find a *double bar line*. This is the musical equivalent of a full-stop.

Time Signatures
At the beginning of the stave, after the clef, you will see two numbers stacked on top of one another – this symbol is known as the *time signature*. It tells you the number of notes of equal value in each bar.

The upper figure tells you the number of beats in a bar and the lower figure indicates what kind of a note has one beat.

For example, the top number (4) indicates four beats per bar and the bottom number (4) indicates that each beat is a crotchet.

Tip
$\frac{4}{4}$ is sometimes written as 𝐂 standing for common time – because it is the most commonly used time signature.

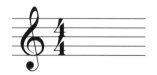

← 4 beats per bar   3 beats per bar →
← A crotchet note gets 1 beat →

In a 4/4 time signature:

𝐨   Semibreve = 4 beats

♩   Minim   = 2 beats

♩   Crotchet   = 1 beat

♪   Quaver   = 1/2 beat

♬   Semiquaver = 1/4 beat

Each of the following bars takes exactly the same time to play (if you keep the speed of the beat the same). What varies are the number of notes (and their duration) played within the bar.

In a 4/4 time signature the largest note value per bar is a semibreve:

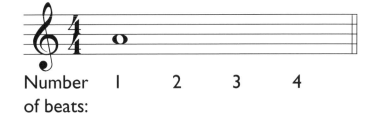

Dividing a semibreve in half creates two minims:

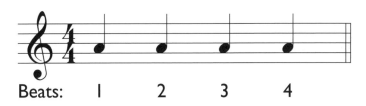

Dividing again creates four crotchets:

Dividing each crotchet creates eight quavers:

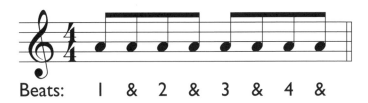

Take a rest!

Silence is just as important as sound in any type of music.

In written music silence is indicated with signs on the stave called rests. Just as the note values tell you the number of beats to hold the note, so rest values tell you the number of beats to remain silent.

This example gives you the most common note values and their matching rests:

> **Tip**
>
> Rests can be thought of as "unplayed notes" and they have to be counted, just as you count the notes you actually play.

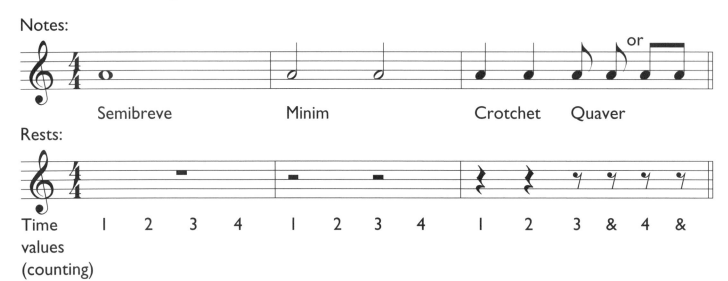

Notes:				
	Semibreve	Minim	Crotchet	Quaver

Rests:										
Time values (counting)	1	2	3	4	1	2	3	4	1	2	3	&	4	&

Charlie Parker and Miles Davis:
The birth of cool

CHECKPOINT
WHAT YOU'VE ACHIEVED SO FAR...

You can now:
- Understand the stave and clef
- Read pitches on the treble clef
- Understand note values and time signatures
- Understand rests and their values

The note **B** is written on the middle line of the Treble Clef.

To play it you need to close only one key with the left hand, L1. Take a deep breath and then play the note, holding it for a few seconds.

Listen to **Track 2** and check that you are matching the sound.

Now play four Bs in a row in a steady rhythm. Try it on your own first, then play with **Track 3** – you will first hear four clicks which indicate the crotchet pulse followed by the four B notes. Listen to the rhythm and then try playing along.

L1

L2   left hand

L3

R1

R2   right hand

R3

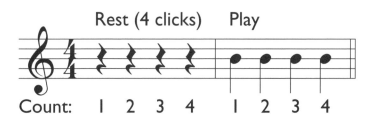

Rest (4 clicks)   Play

Count: 1   2   3   4   1   2   3   4

Tip

When playing, you can keep the beat by counting in your head or by tapping your foot.

Try playing the following exercise on your own, combining crotchet rests with crotchet notes and semibreves:

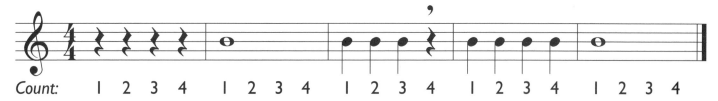

Count: 1 2 3 4   1 2 3 4   1 2 3 4   1 2 3 4   1 2 3 4

This mark **,** indicates breathing places.
Taking breaths is usually done according to musical phrases, so that the flow of the music doesn't stop. Obviously, the best time to take a breath is during a rest, but if there isn't a rest in a suitable place (usually after two or three bars) you'll have to inhale quickly *between* notes. This means that the note before you breathe will be shortened slightly to allow time for you to take a breath.

Breathing

Practise starting and stopping a note – learn to control your diaphragm and breathing so that you get a really smooth, long note. Stop the sound before it begins to drop or quiver (as you run out of breath). In time you'll be able to control the volume and sound quality of each pitch.

Having practised for a while you may find that your jaws are starting to ache and the muscles around your mouth are tightening. This is quite normal! As a basic rule you should play no longer than fifteen minutes after your mouth begins to get sore – any more than that and you could damage your *embouchure* (mouth position). You'll soon find that you'll be able to play for longer periods of time, the more often you practise.

The Tongue

What does the tongue do? It starts notes, ends notes, and dictates whether a note is loud or soft. It plays a leading role in phrasing and is as important to the sax player as drum sticks are to the percussionist!

Tip

Always aim for a really well organised practice session of twenty to forty-five minutes.

This photo shows **A** and the fingering used, adding L2 to L1. Take a deep breath and then play the note, holding it for a few seconds.

You should try to match your sound with **Track 4**.

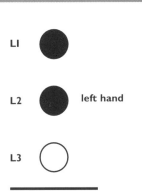

L1 ●

L2 ● left hand

L3 ○

—————

R1 ○

R2 ○ right hand

R3 ○

L1 ●

L2 ● left hand

L3 ●

—————

R1 ○

R2 ○ right hand

R3 ○

Note **G** is played by depressing three keys with the left hand – L1, L2 and L3.

Track 5 gives you the sound of the note.

Now, here's a chance to try out these two new notes. Listen to **Track 6** and count along with the music.

Now try it yourself over the backing on **Track 7**.

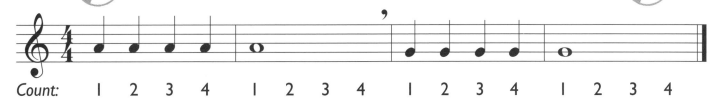

Count: 1   2   3   4   1   2   3   4   1   2   3   4   1   2   3   4

Notes and rests

Here's something to practise involving notes and rests.

1 Play the notes exactly on the first beat of every bar.
2 Count evenly during the rest bars.
3 Make the notes start and end cleanly.

4 Play each note with a smooth, round tone.
5 At the same time, count the beats in your mind.

Listen to **Track 8**.

Now try it yourself with **Track 9**. Remember to count for four before starting!

	Play	Rest	Play	Rest	Play
Count:	1 2 3 4	1 2 3 4	1 2 3 4	1 2 3 4	1 2 3 4

B

A

G

CHECKPOINT

WHAT YOU'VE ACHIEVED SO FAR...

You can now:
• Play the notes **B**, **A**, and **G**
• Play melodies using notes and rests
• Control your breathing

Courtney Pine

Two or more note values can be connected to each other with a curved line called a tie. A tie joins together notes of the same pitch to make a longer note which is the sum of the separate note values.

Try playing these four bars – the note A is held for a total of six counts, while G is held for a total of 5 counts.

Count: 1   2   3   4   1   2   3   4   1   2   3   4   1   2   3   4

We can simplify this example by replacing two crotchet rests with a minim rest.

Ties can also occur within the same bar.
Here, the duration of each note is three beats:

Count: 1   2   3   4   1   2   3   4

The next piece requires you to tongue three crotchet notes in a row and rest for one crotchet. Listen for the four beat clicks on **Track 10** to bring you in.

Count: 1   2   3   4   1   2   3   4

You can play on your own with the backing track on **Track 11**.

Tip

A breath mark is not necessary when there is a rest since that's a good place to breathe anyway.

Speed up your learning!

The next two pieces combine many of the things you have learned so far. Listen to the recordings, while counting and following the music.

Then play the exercises on your own, concentrating on the tone of your instrument. Finally, play along with the backing tracks.

B

A

G

Listen to **Track 12** to hear how this sounds;
and play along with **Track 13**.

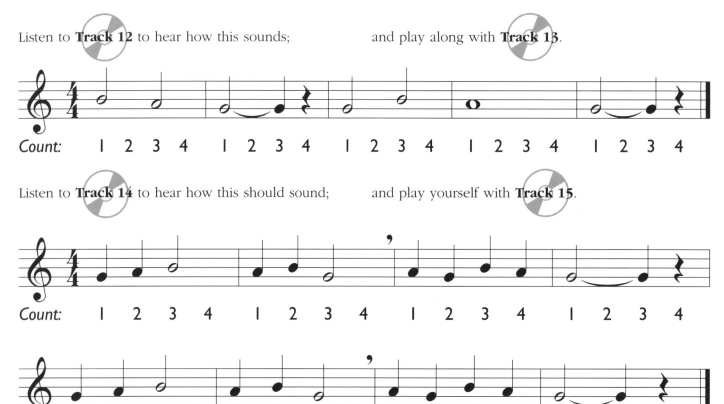

Count: 1   2   3   4   1   2   3   4   1   2   3   4   1   2   3   4   1   2   3   4

Listen to **Track 14** to hear how this should sound;
and play yourself with **Track 15**.

Count: 1   2   3   4   1   2   3   4   1   2   3   4   1   2   3   4

ABSOLUTE BEGINNERS
Alto Saxophone Fingering Chart

THUMB SUPPORT

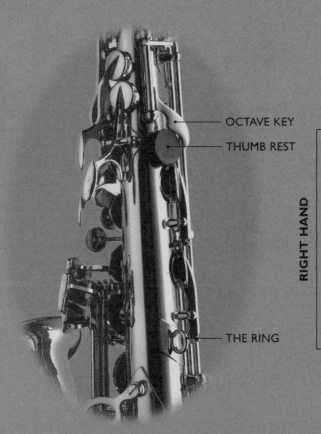

OCTAVE KEY

THUMB REST

THE RING

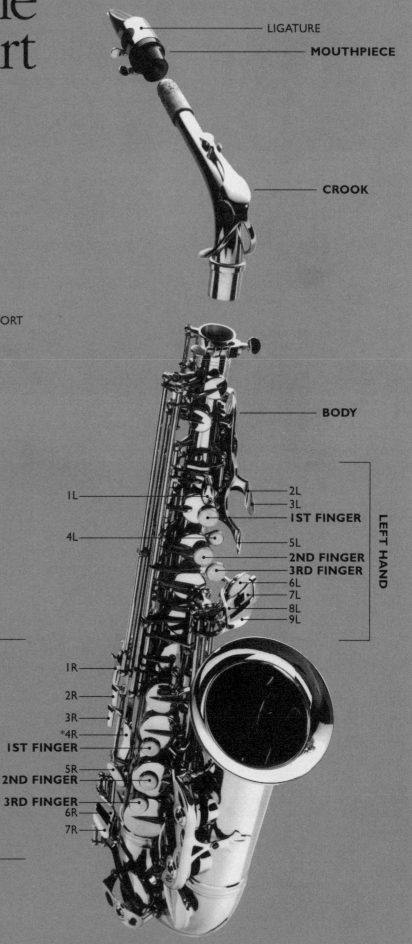

LIGATURE

MOUTHPIECE

CROOK

BODY

1L
2L
3L
1ST FINGER
4L
5L
2ND FINGER
3RD FINGER
6L
7L
8L
9L

LEFT HAND

1R
2R
3R
*4R
1ST FINGER
5R
2ND FINGER
3RD FINGER
6R
7R

RIGHT HAND

*Not fitted on some saxophones

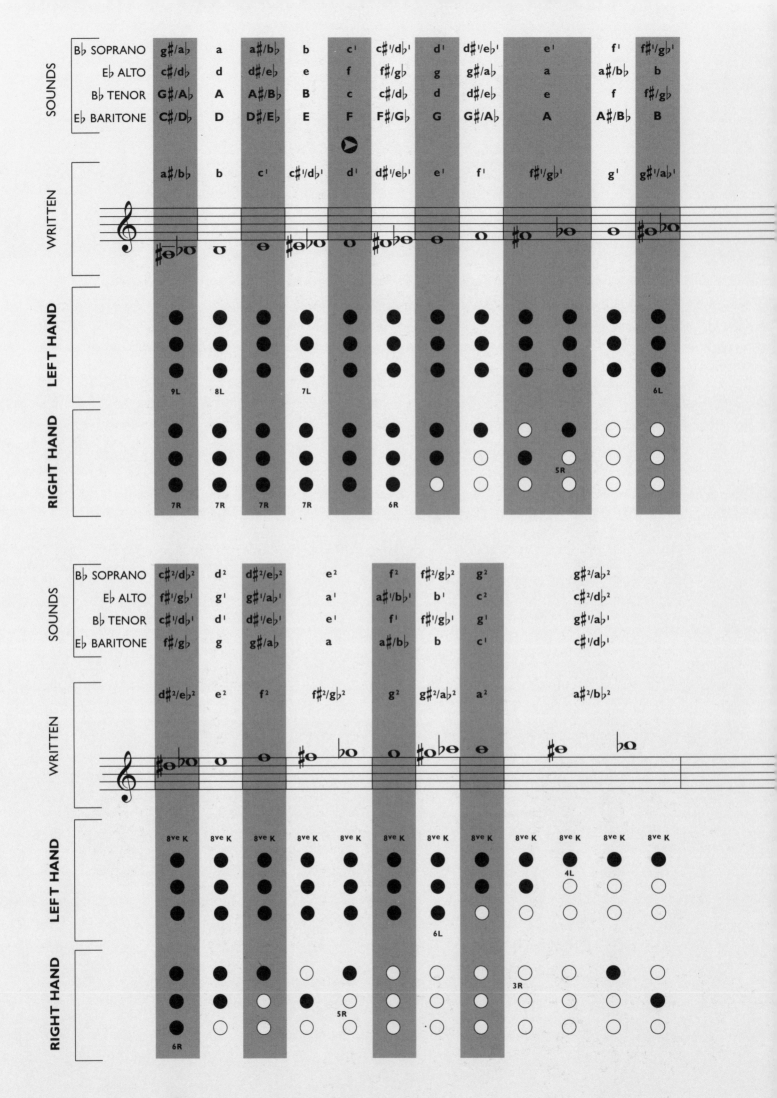

Indicates the lower limit of the best playing range

g¹   g#¹/ab¹   a¹   a#¹/bb¹   b¹   c²
c¹   c#¹/db¹   d¹   d#¹/eb¹   e¹   f¹
g   g#/ab   a   a#/bb   b   c¹
c   c#/db   d   d#/eb   e   f

a¹   a#¹/bb¹   b¹   c²   c#²/db²   d²

4L   3R   2R   8ve K   7L   7R

a²   a#²/bb²   b²   c³   c#³/db³   d³   d#³/eb³
d²   d#²/eb²   e²   f²   f#²/gb²   g²   g#²/ab²
a¹   a#¹/bb¹   b¹   c²   c#²/db²   d²   d#²/eb²
d¹   d#¹/eb¹   e¹   f¹   f#¹/gb¹   g¹   g#¹/ab¹

b²   c³   c#³/db³   d³   d#³/eb³   e³   f³

8ve K   8ve K   8ve K   8ve K   8ve K   8ve K   8ve K   8ve K   8ve K   8ve K

3L   2L 3L   2L 3L   1L   2L 3L 5L   1L

2R   1R   1R

Indicates the upper limit of the best playing range

Transposition

B♭ soprano saxophone sounds a major second below the written pitch. Rule: **Written C sounds B♭**

Written:

Sounds:

E♭ alto saxophone sounds a major sixth below the written pitch. Rule: **Written C sounds E♭**

Written:

Sounds:

B♭ tenor saxophone sounds a major ninth below the written pitch. Rule: **Written C sounds B♭**

Written:

Sounds:

E♭ baritone saxophone sounds a major thirteenth below the written pitch. Rule: **Written C sounds E♭**

Written:

Sounds:

Legato means "joined up" – notes played *legato* should flow into each other and sound lyrical. You can achieve this effect on the saxophone by not tongueing between notes.

A *slur* is a curved line (which looks like a tie) that instructs you to play legato – you'll find it between two or more notes of different pitch. Legato playing must be very smooth, so it's important to keep your breath even and constant.

The next exercise uses both slurs and ties.

Tip

Tie or Slur?

Ties and slurs can sometimes look alike – so how do you tell the difference?

Easy – a tie can only exist between two notes of the same pitch. A slur can only exist between notes of different pitch.

Listen to **Track 16** and play along with **Track 17**.

Here are two more exercises to help you with legato and slurring:

Count, listen, and play along with **Tracks 18** and **19**.

Now try speeding this up a bit! Listen to **Track 20** and then play along with **Track 21**.

Another rhythm

Quavers (or eighth notes) are the shortest notes that you're going to play in this book – they require accurate counting and tongueing.

How To Count Quavers
Quavers split the crotchet beat in half; in a 4/4 bar they are counted like this:

An easy way of remembering the duration of combined quavers and crotchets is (without playing) to call a crotchet 'tea' and two quavers "coffee".

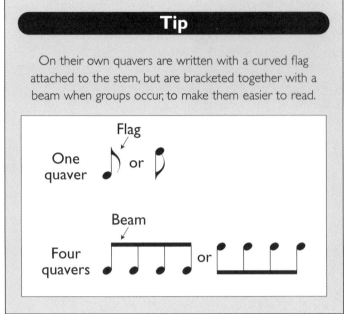
tea   cof-fee

Look at the example below and say the words under the stave rhythmically. Next, clap the line as you say the words. Then play the two bars, keeping a steady beat pulse.

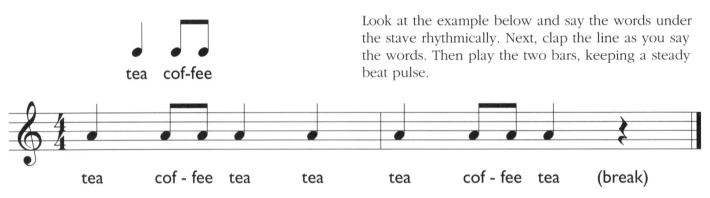

tea   cof - fee tea   tea   tea   cof - fee tea   (break)

Here's a tune full of crotchets and quavers – to practise the rhythm, speak the words (rhythmically); then choose a slow speed and count with a steady beat so you can also focus on your tongueing and fingering. Practise the tune a few times at a slow rhythm until you can speed up and still be accurate. Look out for the *repeat sign* at the end of the piece – listen to **Track 22** to hear how it should sound. Try playing along yourself, with **Track 23**.

Repeats
If you see the sign :‖ at the end of a piece, it means that you are to repeat the entire piece. Sometimes only a section of a piece is to be repeated and you will see the sign ‖: at the beginning, and :‖ at the end of that section.

coffee coffee tea tea coffee coffee tea   coffee coffee tea tea coffee coffee tea

coffee tea coffee tea   tea coffee tea tea   1 2 3   4   1 2 3   4

The speed of a piece of music is called the *tempo*. A calm, lyrical dance would have a slower tempo than a brisk march. The tempo is usually indicated at the beginning of a piece with a descriptive word such as "fast" or "moderate". If no tempo is indicated, play at a speed which is comfortable to you.

However slowly or quickly you play, the note values must remain constant, relative to each other.

Choose a medium slow tempo for the next piece. Think the rhythm to yourself before playing the notes then listen to **Track 24** and play along with **Track 25**.

Al-ou-et-te gen-tile al-ou-et-te al-ou-et-te je te plu-me-rai.

Now play the piece with the slurs as marked – remember that musical phrases written with slurs should be played legato with only the first note

tongued. Tongue all the other pitches clearly. Listen to **Track 26** for a demonstration of how this should sound. Now play along with **Track 27**.

Al-ou-et-te gen-tile al-ou-et-te al-ou-et-te je te plu-me-rai.

CHECKPOINT

WHAT YOU'VE ACHIEVED SO FAR...

You can now:
- Read and count quavers
- Understand repeat signs
- Understand musical tempo

The notes F and C

Here is the note **F**, which you can hear on **Track 28**. It adds one more finger to the G position, this time with the right hand, R1. Play and hold the note F a few times, creating a steady sound. Try to match the quality of sound (the tone) on the recording.

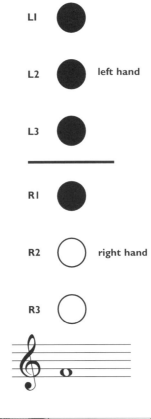

L1 ●
L2 ● left hand
L3 ●

R1 ●
R2 ○ right hand
R3 ○

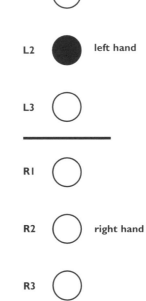

L1 ○
L2 ● left hand
L3 ○

R1 ○
R2 ○ right hand
R3 ○

The note C
This fingering may seem a little unusual – only press down L2 with your left hand and try not to raise fingers L1 and L3 too high.
Listen to the recording of C – **Track 29** – and then play it yourself.

You have now learned how to read and play five notes – **F**, **G**, **A**, **B** and **C**. First listen to the sound of these notes and then play them alone a few times.

This half-scale is demonstrated on **Track 30**.

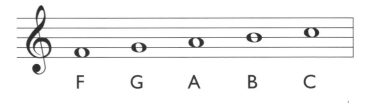

F   G   A   B   C

Before moving on to another piece, try the following patterns. These will help secure the finger positions in your mind.

Listen to the recording, practise on your own keeping each note steady until you feel confident, then play along with the backing track.

Tracks 31 & 32

Moderate

Tracks 33 & 34

Slow

Tracks 35 & 36

Slow

Rocky Road

Now you have a chance to play a whole piece!

You will notice a repeat sign at the end of Bar 8: go back to the beginning and then after the second play through, go on to the rest of the piece.

Always count the beats in your head as you play – the time signature will tell you how many beats there are in each bar and what value to count.
Listen to **Track 37** for a demonstration of this piece.
Then try playing along yourself with **Track 38**.

Rock beat

CHECKPOINT

WHAT YOU'VE ACHIEVED SO FAR...

You can now:
• Play five notes – **F**, **G**, **A**, **B** and **C**

Earlier we showed how notes of the same pitch can be tied together to extend their length. We can achieve the same effect by adding a dot after the note – this increases the value of the note by half and is played as one extended note.

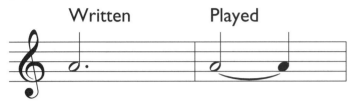

The reason for writing dotted notes in music is to simplify the notation. One dotted note takes up less space – and can be easier to read – than two notes tied together. However, unlike ties which can connect notes in different bars, the value of dotted notes only lasts within a single bar.

Tip

Notice that the time signature occurs just once at the start and then applies for the rest of the piece, unless it is replaced by another (different) time signature.

All of the other note values can be dotted as well, with the dot representing an additional half of the note value. Dots apply to rests in the same way.

The next two pieces include the new notes F and C. You will also be playing

1 Dotted minims – 3 crotchet beats long.
2 Dotted crotchets – $1\frac{1}{2}$ crotchet beats long.
3 Ties (same pitches connected).
4 Slurs (different pitches connected and played legato).

Now try the example below, remembering to count carefully. The demo is on **Track 39**, and you can play along with **Track 40**.

Up or down?

As you may have noticed already, the notes B and C usually have their stems heading downwards (in fact, all higher notes do this). Stem direction simply makes notes easier to read and has no musical effect.

You can hear this next example on **Track 41**. Count to yourself and listen out for the effect of the dotted notes, tied notes and legato slurs.

Fairly Slow

Now try playing along yourself using the backing track on **Track 42**.

Tip

Try writing out the counts underneath or above each bar. This will help you place the different rhythms accurately.

CHECKPOINT

WHAT YOU'VE ACHIEVED SO FAR...

You can now:
• Read and play dotted notes, ties and slurs.

The Note E

This time, add two fingers with the right hand to the G position, so you are now pressing down five keys.

Listen to **Track 43** to hear how E should sound.

LI
L2 left hand
L3
RI
R2 right hand
R3

LI
L2 left hand
L3
RI
R2 right hand
R3

The Note D

Now add the third finger on your right hand to the shape you just made for the note E. Try to keep an even pressure on each key.

Now listen to **Track 44** to hear how D should sound.

Try and match the tone of the notes you hear on the recording.

CHECKPOINT

WHAT YOU'VE ACHIEVED SO FAR...

You can now:
• Play seven notes – **D**, **E**, **F**, **G**, **A**, **B** and **C**

The magnificent seven

You now know seven different notes.
Study the chart below and note how the keys are
pressed down as the notes go down in pitch.

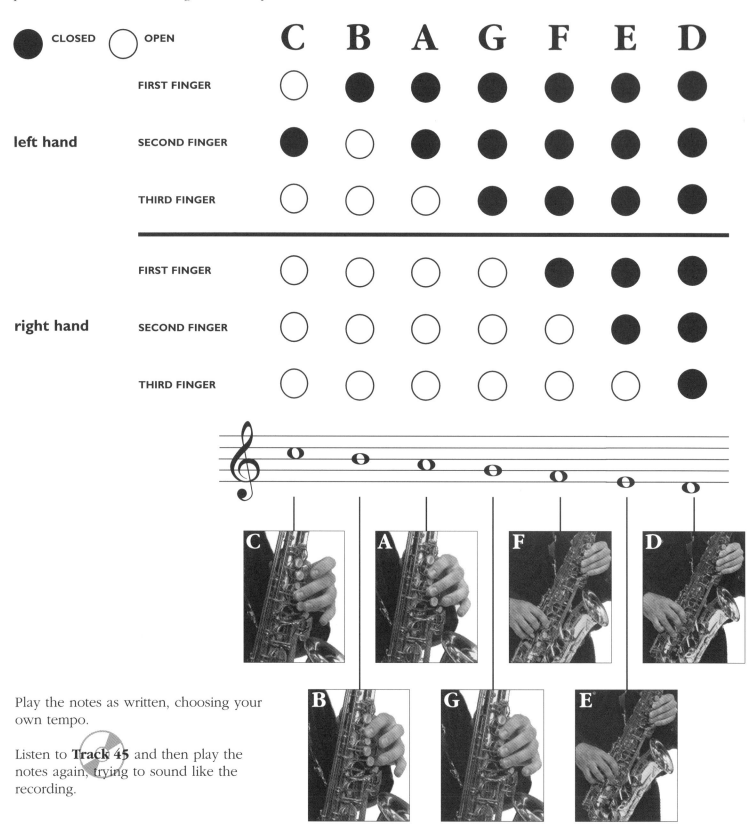

Play the notes as written, choosing your
own tempo.

Listen to **Track 45** and then play the
notes again, trying to sound like the
recording.

To familiarise yourself with D and E play this tune and get comfortable with the new finger positions.

Before playing the next piece, think the rhythms in your mind or clap them, counting aloud.
You can either play the piece first or listen to the recording (**Track 46**), but you'll need to practise this slowly a few times.

The backing track is on **Track 47**.

Remember to keep the slurred notes smooth, and watch out for the last tied note: hold this for five beats.

The octave key

Note names begin with the letters **A**, **B**, **C**, **D**, **E**, **F** and **G** (all of which you now know). This pattern of notes is repeated over and over, throughout the range of the saxophone.

There are eight notes between D and the next D (including the two Ds). The gap between those two Ds (called an *interval*) is called an *octave* (from the Greek word meaning eight).

D E F G A B C D E F G A B C

Two notes spaced an octave apart, called by the same letter name, sound very similar to each other, although one is higher than the other. If two instruments are playing an octave apart it can almost sound like one note playing instead of two.

The saxophone has an *Octave key*. If you press this key down in addition to the fingerings you already know, each note will sound an octave higher. The octave key can be found on the back of your saxophone, just above the thumb rest for your left hand.

Thumb on rest

Thumb on octave key

Jargon Buster

Interval – the distance in pitch between two notes

Octave – two notes separated by an interval of eight letter names

Octave Key Technique

Follow these simple guidelines to ensure a good octave key technique:

1 Place your thumb on the thumb rest with a small part of the end of the thumb over the octave key.

2 Depress the octave key with a flick motion, bending the joint of your thumb.

3 Keep your thumb on the thumb rest at all times – make sure it doesn't lift off.

The fingering for this D is just like the lower D, except that you also press the octave key. This is true for notes from D up to high C: same fingering plus octave key.

Listen to **Track 48** and play the new D yourself.

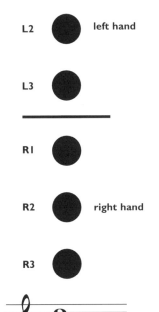

Practise this tune – slowly at first. Note that the melody will be played twice because of the repeat sign. Listen to **Track 49** for a slow demonstration.

The backing track is on **Track 50**.

Once you're happy at a slow tempo, listen to **Track 51** and try speeding it up!

This example uses exactly the same notes, but written in quavers instead of crotchets. You can play along yourself, with **Track 52**.

Double up!

You have now effectively doubled the number of notes you can play! Let's play through each of those notes with **Track 53**, listening carefully to the octave interval sounds for each note.

[*Use octave key]

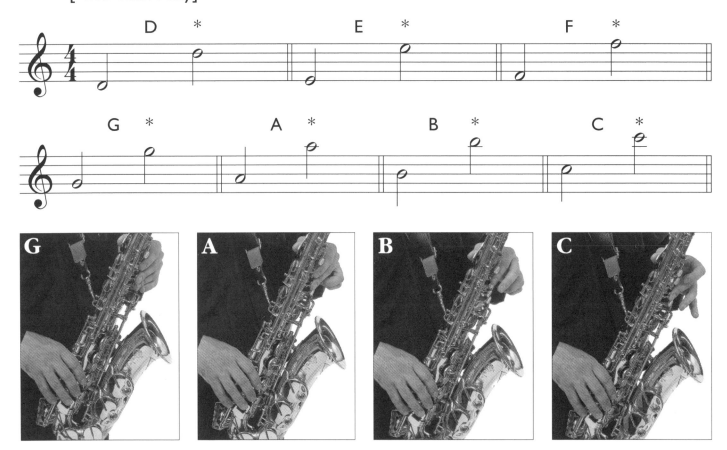

CHECKPOINT

WHAT YOU'VE ACHIEVED SO FAR...

You can now:
• Use the octave key with all seven notes.

An *accidental* is a sign placed in front of a note, which shows that the pitch of that note has been altered. You know the notes F and G:

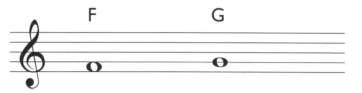

The difference in pitch (the interval) between these notes is one tone. Many of the notes you have played have been one tone apart. For example:

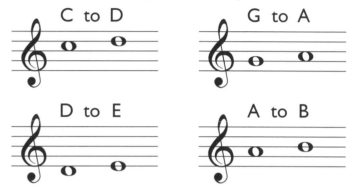

Play these intervals (including F to G) and listen to the difference in their pitches. After you have done that – read on.

Here are the three accidental signs – sharp, flat and natural:

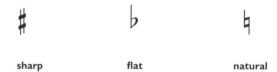

Sharpening a note means increasing its pitch by half a tone – called a semitone. Flattening a note means lowering its pitch by a semitone. A natural sign cancels a sharp or flat that has appeared immediately before, restoring the note to it's original pitch.

Tip

Accidentals are placed on the same line or space just before the first note they affect, and they apply until the end of the bar unless cancelled by a natural sign.

Sharpen up!

Exactly half way between F and G there is another note a semitone distance from both. This note can be called **F sharp** (one semitone higher than F) or G flat (one semitone lower than G), depending on which is easier to read at the time.

Here is F sharp / G flat.

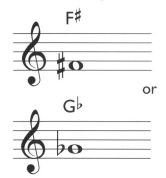

Adding the octave key, the notes are written like this:

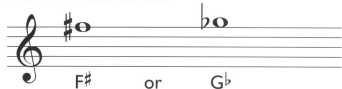

Play both the low and the high F sharps and listen to them on **Tracks 54 & 55**.

The note **C sharp** (or D flat) is written and played like this:

Listen to **Track 56** to hear what C sharp sounds like. You might recognise this note – it was the first note you played, back on page 12!

L1 ●
L2 ● left hand
L3 ●

R1 ○
R2 ● right hand
R3 ○

L1 ○
L2 ○ left hand
L3 ○

R1 ○
R2 ○ right hand
R3 ○

When a section of music begins with only a clef and a time signature, this means it is in the key of C major. Sometimes, when we want to play in different keys, some notes will need to be sharp or flat all the way through a piece.

Rather than use *accidentals*, (which would have to appear in almost every bar) we can use a *key signature*, which appears at the beginning of each stave. It contains sharp or flat signs indicating which notes need to be altered to create the right key.

For example, if the note B is to be played flat throughout the key signature is:

If the note F is to be played ♯ throughout, the key signature would look like this:

The next two tunes have key signatures with a ♯ in them – so all F's that appear in these pieces should be played as F♯s.

Tip

The accidentals of a key signature apply to the note at all octaves.

1 2 3   1 2 3   etc.

Tip

These pieces also introduce a new time signature in which there are only three crotchet beats – count 1, 2, 3 for each bar. This time signature is sometimes known as waltz time. **3/4**

Remember to use F♯ every time you see the note F!

This next example, "Rainbow Waltz" is demonstrated on **Track 57**. Listen to this, practise slowly, and then play along with **Track 58**.

Rainbow Waltz

The scale

You're now ready to play your first scale. Scales are great for developing your skill on the instrument – practise them regularly and soon you'll be playing with greater fluency.

The most common scale is the major scale, consisting of eight notes spanning an octave. Here is C major, a scale which has no sharps or flats:

C major scale

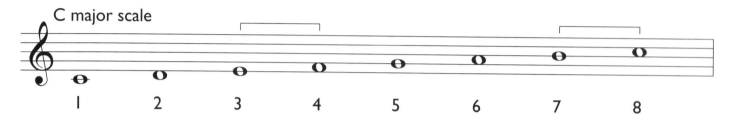

Looking at this scale you will see that E and F and B and C are bracketed. All the other notes are a tone apart, but these pairs are only a semitone apart.

These notes are numbered 3-4, 7-8 – these numbers, or degrees, of the major scale must always be a semitone apart, regardless of the note names.

Scale of D major
Study this scale of D major and then play it, listening to **Track 59**.

In this scale the semitone intervals are F♯ to G (3-4) and C♯ to D (7-8).

D major scale

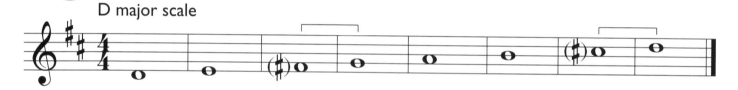

Practise slowly at first and try to play in one breath to the top of the scale, making all the notes sound clearly. Now play the scale both up and down, as demonstrated on **Track 60**.

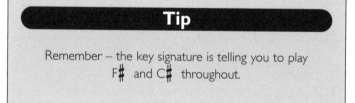

Tip

Remember – the key signature is telling you to play F♯ and C♯ throughout.

Scale of G major
Another scale you can play is G major – this has only one accidental in the key signature, F♯.

You can hear this on **Track 61**.

G major scale

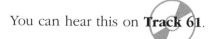

Tip

It can help to practise the major scale of a piece (which you can tell from its key signature) before playing the piece.

Now here's your chance to play two complete pieces! You will be using everything you have learnt in this book. Remember to repeat both pieces twice, and try to produce a smooth, controlled tone from your saxophone.

"Cut Loose" is in G major – so remember those F♯s – and is at a moderate speed. Listen to **Track 62**, and play along with **Track 63**.

Cut Loose

The final piece, "Swing Blues" is in D major (remember to use C♯ and F♯) and has an up-tempo beat.

You can hear this demonstrated on **Track 64**, and you can play along on your own, with the backing track, on **Track 65**.

Swing Blues

Congratulations!

In a very short space of time you've covered a lot of ground – you're already well on your way to playing proficiently. You've learnt a lot about how to hold your saxophone, how to breathe properly and how to produce notes. You've also learnt a lot about music – how to read notation and rhythm, and how to understand accidentals and key signatures.

A Touch of Frost **theme** Barbara Thompson
Lily Was Here Candy Dulfer
One Step Beyond Madness
Songbird Kenny G
Young Americans David Bowie

Careless Whisper George Michael
Girl from Ipanema Stan Getz
Will You Hazel O'Connor
The Two of Us Bill Withers (Sax: Grover Washington)
Papa's Got A Brand New Bag James Brown

Barbara Thompson

Grover Washington

Candy Dulfer

David Bowie

After use cleaning routine

Before putting your instrument away, spend a short time wiping it down and cleaning it outside with a handtowel-sized cloth. The inside must be dried since your breath, being warm and moist, will cause a small amount of liquid to condense in the body of the instrument.

It is highly recommended that you purchase a pad-saver. This is made of absorbent material with a rigid wire at its core which is the same length as the saxophone. It is pushed into the instrument and stays there when not in use, soaking up any remaining moisture.

Remove the mouthpiece from the neck and wipe it dry with a small cloth used only for the mouthpiece. The reed must be dried and stored immediately.

Use a crook swab to carefully clean inside the crook and instrument body.

You can now assemble, dismantle, clean and maintain your saxophone!

Further reading

Now you're ready to move onto more advanced material – investigate some of the titles below; they'll help you continue to develop your technique, and will introduce you to some of the great saxophone repertoire that you'll be able to play. See the Music Sales Catalogue for the full list of titles.

The Big Easy

This best-selling series, based on popular tunes and light classics, is specially arranged for the beginner-intermediate player. There are separate books for the Alto and Tenor saxophones.

The Big Easy Classics Collection
AM 936750
The Big Easy Essential Home Library
AM 936650
The Big Easy from the Beatles to the Blues
AM 936705

Saxmania!

This superb series offers an incredible wealth of great tunes in a wide range of styles. Arranged for Eb and Bb saxophones with chord symbols for both instruments.

Saxmania! Blues Greats
'Fever', 'Summertime Blues', 'The Lonesome Road', 'Memphis Blues' plus many more.
AM 90099

Saxmania! Great Solos
Includes 'Baker Street', 'Starsky & Hutch', 'Lily Was Here', and 'Careless Whisper'.
AM 90123

Saxmania! Jazz Hits
Includes 'Take Five', 'Minnie the Moocher', 'Round Midnight', 'Tuxedo Junction' and many more.
AM 78254

John Coltrane Solos

Artist Transcriptions

Features 26 of John Coltrane's most important solos. Includes 'Round Midnight', 'All Blues', 'Blue Train', 'My Favorite Things', 'Giant Steps' and many more.
HLE00673233

George Gershwin for Saxophone

Twenty-four memorable Gershwin tunes arranged for saxophone by Robin de Smet, including 'But Not For Me', 'Embraceable You', 'I Got Rhythm', and 'The Man I Love'. Includes chord symbols.
AM 68479

Stan Getz: Transcriptions for Saxophone

Artist transcriptions of melodies and solos by Greg Fishman. Includes biography and style analysis. Titles include 'All The Things You Are', 'Body and Soul', 'Early Autumn', and 'The Girl from Ipanema'.
AM 931535